Handbook
on CEO–Board

Relations and
Responsibilities

George R. Boggs

Foreword by Constance M. Carroll

Community College Press®
A division of the American Association of Community Colleges

The American Association of Community Colleges (AACC) is the primary advocacy organization for the nation's community colleges. The association represents more than 1,100 two-year, associate degree–granting institutions and more than 11 million students. AACC promotes community colleges through six strategic action areas: national and international recognition and advocacy, learning and accountability, leadership development, economic and workforce development, connectedness across AACC membership, and international and intercultural education. Information about AACC and community colleges may be found at www.aacc.nche.edu.

Design: Brian Gallagher Design
Editor: Deanna D'Errico
Printer: Kirby Lithographic

Community College Press
American Association of Community Colleges
One Dupont Circle, NW
Suite 410
Washington, DC 20036

Printed in the United States of America

ISBN 0-87117-370-0

Early Reviews

George Boggs has written the handbook I was looking for and could not find when I first became a CEO. The CEO–board relationship is extremely critical to the successful governance of community colleges, and Boggs has addressed all aspects of that relationship.

—*Patricia Stanley*
President (Retired), Frederick Community College

This user-friendly guide takes a practical, no-nonsense approach to describing the delicate balance and the critical factors affecting CEO–board relations.

—*Henry Shannon*
Chancellor, St. Louis Community Colleges, and Chair, AACC Board of Directors, 2004–2005

In *Governing Boards: Their Nature and Nurture* (1989), Cyril Houle stated, "A good board is a victory, not a gift." CEOs who appreciate and support their boards and respect and reinforce the contributions and strengths of each trustee will be more likely to achieve the victory. The knowledge and experience captured in this book provides CEOs with essential tools to help their boards be great.

—*Cindra J. Smith*
Director, Education Services, Community College League of California

This handbook is an outstanding presentation of the roles of CEOs and boards in community colleges. It clarifies and illuminates an often-discussed topic and outlines a recipe for success for those engaged in a professional dynamic that requires a keen understanding of human interactions.

—*Jerry Sue Thornton*
President, Cuyahoga Community College

George Boggs has written a down-to-earth, real-life rendering of the vital relationship between trustees and the college CEO, with the subtlety and thoroughness that only experience can bring.

—*Eduardo J. Padron*
President, Miami Dade College

As one who has worked with dozens of community college boards and presidents, I can't think of a more useful *vade mecum* for a new trustee or CEO. I wouldn't want to be either a trustee or a president until I had read this book.

—*Gary Davis*
Principal, Board Solutions

The difference between a dynamic "serve the people" college and one that plods along without much progress often depends on how well the trustees and the president work together. George Boggs has written a thoughtful working guide that encourages boards and presidents to engage in a productive, positive relationship that serves the best interests of students and communities.

—*David H. Ponitz*
President Emeritus, Sinclair Community College

This handbook is well organized and structured; the writing clear, coherent, and concise. It will be of tremendous use for current and aspiring CEOs as well as board members.

—*Alfredo G. de los Santos, Jr.*
Research Professor, Arizona State University

This handbook is vintage Boggs: wise, fair, and clear—and grounded in the reality of his own experience. It is the best primer of its kind and should be required reading for every CEO and every trustee in the nation's community colleges.

—*Terry O'Banion*
President Emeritus and Senior League Fellow, League for Innovation in the Community College

Contents

Lessons Learned

Foreword

Although many individuals and groups are involved in community college governance, planning, and decision making, at the heart of the process is the relationship—both functional and personal—between the CEO and the governing board. The CEO and the board not only have a professional reporting relationship but also function as partners in implementing the college's mission and in ensuring the quality of its services and programs. Both have responsibilities that are distinctive to their respective roles, but they also have shared responsibilities and, in some instances, roles for which distinctions may not be clear.

To some degree, the CEO–board relationship is shaped by the nature of the college itself: whether it is public, private, or proprietary; urban, suburban, or rural; large or small and configured as a single college, a multicampus college, or a multicollege district. Other influences include whether the CEO is a president, superintendent-president, or chancellor or the college is governed by an elected or appointed board.

In recent decades, community college governance has been further complicated by other factors. Externally, legislation at federal and state levels has become increasingly intrusive in the decisions made by college leaders, as efforts to prescribe both methodologies and outcomes have proliferated. Internally, colleges may also be pressured to respond to issues that are raised by consultants or that emerge from collective bargaining. Accreditation and funding agency requirements, interest group agendas, the evolving socioeconomic demographics of local communities, and the ever-changing needs of students further complicate decision making. The CEO–board relationship is challenged by these and other polycentric pressures, making it more necessary than ever to clarify and properly define roles and functions to ensure effective governance.

Irrespective of the nature, mission, location, or configuration of the community college, some overarching principles and considerations are common to an effective CEO–board relationship. The *Handbook on CEO–Board Relations and Responsibilities* clarifies the dynamics and challenges of this leadership partnership. Above all, it is an insightful and practical guide to the best practices that CEOs and boards should consider and pitfalls they should avoid in dealing with key issues such as hiring and evaluating CEOs, balancing responsibility, and communicating. The *Handbook* is written in a clear and engaging manner. Every page reflects the author's experience as a CEO, an accreditor, a student of leadership, and someone who views community colleges from a broad, national perspective.

Although community colleges share a common mission, they are also highly diverse, reflecting the diversity of their constituents—students and communities. CEOs and governing boards must represent and be accountable to a broad segment of a public that has different interests, needs, and levels of engagement. Therefore, although developing successful relationships between CEOs and boards is important in any organization, it is of key importance in the community college setting. For that reason, the *Handbook on CEO–Board Relations and Responsibilities* should become part of the working library of all CEOs and board members who are committed to providing an effective leadership team for their community colleges and the local communities that depend on them.

Constance M. Carroll, Chancellor
San Diego Community College District

Preface and Acknowledgments

The purpose of this handbook is to provide guidance to community college CEOs who report to governing boards. The intention is to offer useful and successful strategies to CEOs for building and maintaining positive relationships with and among their boards and for improving their effectiveness in meeting their governance responsibilities. The book includes information about the approaches that many effective and experienced CEOs use to maintain positive relationships, as well as those used to improve relationships and behavior. Although the primary audience is CEOs, the handbook should be equally valuable to other administrators who work with boards, to those who aspire to the position of CEO, and to trustees who want to learn more about the relationship between boards and CEOs from the latter's perspective.

For those who wish to refer to specific topics, the handbook is organized into sections that can be read in any order. Sixteen seasoned CEOs and governance consultants have contributed advice that appears throughout the book. The words that seem to appear most frequently in these good-practice vignettes are *communication, trust, respect,* and *openness.* The appendixes contain sample policies and evaluation tools, as well as a sample code of ethics. Numerous state and national trustee associations also provide technical assistance in developing policies and instruments. In particular, the Association of Community College Trustees (ACCT), cited throughout this handbook, has many resources listed on its Web site.

———◆———

I wish to acknowledge the contributions of the many people who read the manuscript and made valuable suggestions that I incorporated into this handbook. In particular, Gary Davis, Alfredo de los Santos, Terry O'Banion, Dave Ponitz, and Cindra Smith provided valuable insights. I have been a student of leadership and governance for more than 35 years and am grateful to the many trustees and CEOs who have been my instructors over the years. The trustees to whom I have reported for more than 20 years have been my most influential teachers in the important area of CEO–board relations and responsibilities. The trustees and CEOs who have made numerous presentations at American Association of Community Colleges (AACC) and ACCT conventions and institutes of the Presidents Academy have also influenced my thinking.

I wish to thank the CEOs and consultants who contributed their seasoned advice to this book in the form of lessons learned: Priscilla J. Bell, David Buettner, Pamila Fisher, Rufus Glaspar, Brice Harris, Zelema Harris, E. Jan Kehoe, Alberto L. Lorenzo, James H. McCormick, Wayne Newton, Charlene Nunley, Gwendolyn Stephenson, Robert J. Templin, Pamela Transue, J. William Wenrich, and P. Anthony Zeiss.

Constance Carroll, author of the foreword, chaired the Accrediting Commission for Junior and Community Colleges in the Western Association of Schools and Colleges during part of my tenure on the commission. Ineffective CEO–board relations were one of the most frequent concerns of the commission in reviewing accreditation reports during this period. The commissioners' discussions had an impact on my reasoning and my belief in the need for a handbook to help CEOs improve both relationships and effectiveness.

I appreciate the willingness of the Palomar Community College District to share its policies and instruments on ethics and evaluation, which were developed when I served as superintendent/president. These are included in the appendixes.

Finally, I would like to thank my wife, Ann, for her careful reading of the manuscript and suggestions to improve the text. She has been my most consistent supporter and chief editor for nearly 40 years.

Chapter 1

Introduction

Community college CEOs—presidents, superintendent/presidents, or chancellors—consistently rate developing and maintaining positive and productive relationships with their boards of trustees as one of the most important but challenging aspects of their jobs. From a broader perspective, the real challenge for CEOs who report to college or district governing boards is to assist their boards in becoming as effective as they can be. How trustees relate to each other and to the CEO, and how the CEO relates to the trustees is of great consequence. If those relationships are positive, they set the stage for successful governance and leadership; if they are negative, the college can suffer, and the CEO's efficacy can be hampered. CEOs should become students of trusteeship, reading appropriate publications and attending conferences with their trustees. The CEO is the person who is often in the best position to influence the board's performance and relationships—and an effective board will provide the support necessary for the CEO to lead successfully.

A governing board is more than the sum of its individual members. Interactions among board members and between the CEO and trustees make boards dynamic and complex. Different perspectives can provide the environment necessary for making the most informed decisions as long as differences are handled respectfully. Ideally, CEOs and their boards should be seen as a team whose members share common philosophies and objectives (Boggs, 1995b, p. 28). Unfortunately, stories abound of problems among trustees or between CEOs and their boards. Sometimes CEOs come to view their boards as a necessary evil rather than as a valuable group that brings an external perspective to the governance of the college. They may look for ways to manage their boards rather than seeing themselves and their boards as a team that provides direction for a complex enterprise. Building and strengthening these relationships are essential but often not very visible components of the CEO's job—unless the relationship deteriorates.

Improving poor relationships or changing entrenched behavior is not as easy as maintaining positive relationships and behaviors. Some problems are so deeply rooted that they defy resolution, but the experiences of successful CEOs show that workable approaches do exist to avoid or resolve problems and strengthen effectiveness. It may seem counterintuitive to a new CEO that CEOs, rather than the boards they work for, are responsible for developing and maintaining these relationships. Yet trustees often look to their CEOs for advice on matters of governance and board development. Smith (2000, p. 67) has pointed out that CEOs provide essential leadership and guidance to their boards and that the link between boards and their CEOs is interdependent rather than hierarchical.

Trustees, of course, share the responsibility for maintaining effective relationships. State and national trustee association meetings and conferences usually devote workshop sessions to helping board members better understand CEOs and improve their relationships with them. For leaders to understand how they can effectively improve CEO–board relationships, it is necessary to first understand what boards are, how they function, and why they are important to a college—the purpose of the next chapter.

Chapter 2
Definitions and Structure

THE BOARD

Boards of trustees or governing boards act on behalf of the owners of colleges to ensure that they are operating efficiently and in agreement with their mission. The appointing body or the voting public entrusts the college's property and the interests of current and future students and employees to these boards. For public community colleges, the owners are the residents of the state and geographic district that the college serves. The CEO reports to the board and is responsible for carrying out the policies established by the board.

THE CHAIR

The board chair is responsible for chairing meetings and ensuring that business is accomplished with order and efficiency. Although the CEO interacts with all board members, the relationship between the chair and the CEO is special and requires open communication. In some colleges, the tradition of a strong chair changes the relationship that CEOs have with board members. Agreements between the chair and CEO may require that communications to board members be channeled through the chair rather than directly to trustees; the board may designate the chair rather than the CEO to speak on its behalf. This level of involvement for a board chair, however, is uncommon because it is very time consuming. More commonly, the CEO is the point of contact for both the trustees and the public.

A new CEO needs to find out from the board what is expected in relationships with the chair. Dominating board chairs are less likely to occur when the position rotates, either by policy or by practice, and CEOs can usually shape how they interact with both the chair and other members of the board. An experienced retreat facilitator can also help to clarify roles and recommend effective communications. CEOs, of course, are wise to remain uninvolved in the board's selection of officers, especially the chair, except to answer questions and to explain the requirements of the positions.

MAINTAIN AN OPEN FEEDBACK LOOP
Priscilla J. Bell
President, Highline Community College

An open feedback loop best describes the model of CEO–board interaction at Highline Community College: The board members and I are both teachers and learners. Half of my role as CEO is external, both locally and nationally. I gather intelligence to keep the board informed and create opportunities for them to connect with service groups, get involved in advocacy activities, and take part in legislative and business relations. These relationships and activities, in turn, help the board with their primary focus, which is setting policy for the college. The board also takes full advantage of development opportunities to gain exposure to best practices such as ACCT performance self-evaluations, orientations, and conferences.

The board expects me to make this a good place to learn and work, so the other half of my time is devoted to internal issues and maintaining a positive campus culture. Together, the board and I have instituted a number of faculty/staff climate initiatives to participate in campus events and foster what we refer to as the "Highline spirit."

COMMITTEES

The small boards (nine or fewer members) most commonly found in public community colleges can usually operate as a committee of the whole and often do not need to divide into committees. Sometimes, however, small boards have nontrustee community advisory committees or internal college committees that provide recommendations as a way of including more points of view on issues. When committees are a part of the board's structure, CEOs and their staffs generally provide support and advice. They have the responsibility to help committees develop agendas that focus on setting policies and evaluating progress. CEOs may have to caution board members against letting their committees become too specialized and concerned about one aspect of the college at the expense of the entire institution. The committees' purpose should be to advise the board, not the college's staff: CEOs must guard against the risk that small boards, as well as standing committees of large boards, will drift from focusing on policy issues to focusing on administrative decisions. For boards that operate with a committee structure, assessment of the roles and responsibilities of committees should be a part of every orientation and evaluation of the board.

Both small and large boards have potential disadvantages. If a board has more than 10 members, it may be difficult to create an environment that allows trustees to deliberate on issues in depth and to feel personally involved. With larger boards, meetings may be less frequent because they are more difficult to schedule. There may be a tendency for the executive committee to assume more responsibilities of large boards. Small boards, on the other hand, may not be able to reflect a sufficient variety of perspectives and, therefore, may lack the depth necessary to deal wisely with the issues confronting the college.

Although CEOs cannot determine the size of the board, they can mitigate some of the potential problems with boards that are either very large or very small. By establishing an appropriate committee structure—and with proper precautions and consistent reminders from the CEO about appropriate responsibilities—it is usually possible to divide large boards into a suitable number of smaller groups in which the members are actively involved and able to deliberate appropriately. Small boards can expand their vision by receiving advice from college or community advisory committees.

MEETINGS AND AGENDA

Although the board is responsible for preparing and conducting its own meetings, the task of preparing the agenda for board meetings is an important responsibility for the CEO. Agendas should address priorities that the CEO and trustees develop together over time, perhaps emanating from study sessions or retreats; agendas should not consist simply of lists of routine action items for approval. In colleges that have strong board chairs, the chair may also be involved in developing the agenda. Members of the CEO's executive team and staff do most of the technical work of preparing the agenda and gathering the backup materials. It is important to gather and distribute the materials in time to meet the requirements of public notification and allow board members to review and study the issues.

Trustees and the CEO should welcome and encourage the involvement of students, employees, and residents of the district when discussing agenda items and consider their views when deliberating. The board should also set aside time on the meeting agenda for public comment. Alternatively, comments regarding agenda items may be heard as the board takes up these items. Some boards have policies that require non–board members to submit written requests to the CEO before addressing the board or place time limits on individual presentations. CEOs and boards can use these policies to control meetings, but they must be careful not to restrict public comment. To avoid violating both the public trust and open meeting laws, board members should not engage in lengthy discussions about items not on the agenda.

Agenda items may seem to provide an opportunity for board members to take isolated and unrelated actions. However, it is important for the actions of the board to fit into the overall mission and long-range goals of the college. Retreats or planning meetings give the board members an opportunity to think about the big picture, and CEOs should use these occasions to help trustees understand how their actions at board meetings address the college's mission.

A FORMULA FOR SUCCESS
James H. McCormick
Chancellor, Minnesota State Colleges and Universities

Higher education governance can be a tough game. Even if you play it well, practice hard, and follow all the rules, management may carry a different view. Most of the time, if a CEO does not see eye to eye with the board, it is simply because that CEO failed to communicate face to face. My formula for putting CEOs on a foolproof track for success with their governing boards is as follows.

- It is essential to acknowledge the importance of board members. These volunteers give a lot for very little, especially those in the public sector. Many are community leaders who have been chosen by a governor and confirmed by a state's Senate, and they deserve recognition. Look for opportunities to acknowledge their gifts of time and talent.
- The board expects a CEO's leadership to be clear, focused, and strong, but the CEO must always remember what his or her role is and never forget who is in charge. CEOs are usually hired by the governing board.
- The unexpected can sometimes be pleasant, but oftentimes not. Board members should never be surprised by a CEO's action, an occurrence in the system office, or something out of the ordinary on campus. A heads up is as easy as a phone call.
- CEOs should give the board their best: personal integrity, genuine interest, thoughtful planning, and capable leadership. There can be no shirking when it comes to being a good public servant.
- Communicate, communicate, communicate. Don't be a pest, but stay in touch with the board chair and trustees.

Chapter 3
Responsibilities

OVERVIEW

It is important for CEOs to help their boards understand their roles and just how important they are for the success of the college. Trustees also need to know how their roles and responsibilities for effective oversight and governance differ from and interface with the administrative and leadership roles of the CEO and the college staff. A good overview of board roles and responsibilities can be found on ACCT's Web site under Center for Effective Governance and in *Trusteeship in Community Colleges* (Smith, 2000, pp. 15–48). Smith points out that effective boards act as a unit; represent the common good; set policy direction; employ, support, and evaluate the CEO; define policy standards for college operations; monitor institutional performance; create a positive climate, support and advocate the interests of the institution; and lead as a thoughtful, educated team (2000, p. 17). ACCT provides a comprehensive guide to resources for community college trustees that should be reviewed by all CEOs who report to boards.

DEVELOPING POLICY

Board members set policy acting as a unit and relying on the information they receive in agendas and meetings; the CEO and staff provide much of the necessary information. Although conventional wisdom is that policy development is the prerogative of the board and administering those policies is the business of the CEO and the staff, in actual practice, trustees usually expect the CEO to recommend policies for the board's approval. Because the board relies on the CEO to implement its policies, trustees cannot capably set policy in isolation from the CEO and the staff. Board members need to be briefed on how policy recommendations are brought to their attention. In colleges that have strong traditions of faculty and staff participation, internal committees and constituencies study thoroughly all policy change recommendations before they are brought to the board.

    The CEO should be prepared to make a recommendation on proposed policy changes in every case, and the board should be aware that agenda items requiring action usually have been researched and reviewed thoroughly by the CEO and the college's professional staff. Board members should be cautioned against taking action on items that are brought to their attention by special interests and that have not undergone such a review by the CEO and staff. In bringing recommendations to the board, CEOs should include the following information:

- the process used to develop the recommendation
- reasons why action should be taken
- pertinent background data
- expected impact on the college and the community
- implications for student learning
- fiscal implications
- related laws and current policies

✲ Lessons Learned

MAINTAIN TRUST
P. Anthony Zeiss
President, Central Piedmont Community College

No board member can abide by a CEO he or she distrusts, and no CEO can abide by trustees he or she distrusts. Once either a CEO or trustee, especially a chair, violates trust, it is time to begin a new CEO search. It is important for CEOs to always remember that they work both with and at the pleasure of the board. At the end of the day, boards rightly judge CEOs by what has been accomplished toward the vision and mission of the college. It is also important that CEOs keep their boards informed but not abuse their time. I make it a point to talk about policy direction, any major item that might affect the image of the college, and the budget. Like CEOs, trustees do not like surprises. Annual board retreats are the single most important relationship-building event for CEOs and boards.

MONITORING PROGRESS

CEOs are responsible for keeping the board informed through regular reports about policy issues and their implementation. These reports enable boards to monitor or gauge the degree to which the board's previous directions on policy have been satisfied, by providing information about performance against preestablished and agreed-on criteria. A data-driven institutional effectiveness program that includes benchmarks for assessing progress toward institutional goals can be the basis for a good monitoring system. The CEO and staff should design the program, based on the board's priorities.

Monitoring reports assist boards in ensuring that a college is fulfilling its mission. Summaries of accreditation reports and state board reports can provide useful information about a college's performance; reports by outside auditing firms can provide valuable information about the college's financial operations, investment strategies, and fiscal solvency. The board should not, however, confuse requests for the kind of information contained in monitoring reports with requests for information unrelated to measuring progress toward accomplishing goals. The board should be aware that every request it or others make, including calls for information and reports, has a cost to the college. When the costs cannot be justified, boards need to act to protect the college from unnecessary expenses caused by excessive requests for information.

RECRUITING, HIRING, AND RETAINING CEOs

The board's policies can be implemented only through the CEO, and the board depends on the CEO to provide it with the information it needs to govern effectively. Thus, one of the most important tasks a board may be called on to perform is to hire a new CEO—or renegotiate a contract with an existing CEO. Furthermore, as the number of community college CEOs poised to retire in the next 10 years increases, so does the competition for candidates, thus making the recruitment process more challenging (1989). Fortunately, many resources are available to assist boards in their recruitment efforts. These include materials from state and national trustee associations, professional consultants, and AACC's Executive Search partnership (go to www.aacc.nche.edu/execsearch).

In general, good hiring decisions are those that result in a good match between a CEO and a board—that is, the CEO's and the board's vision and understanding of respective roles are compatible, and they are congruent with the mission of the college. From the board's perspective,

> Hiring a new executive—especially for the top job—is a critical intervention in the life and development of an organization. Educational requirements, desired experience, and skill sets are all important in the search process—but far more important are the elements that ensure a fit with the culture and style of the organization. Accurate assessment of the candidate's leadership characteristics and personal qualities is key to making the right choice so that the organization will grow and flourish. (AACC Executive Search, 2006)

From the CEO's perspective, accepting a position that is not a good fit just to become a CEO or to get away from a bad situation usually results in a troubled and short tenure.

Terms of the CEO's employment should always be specified in a written contract that, preferably, has been reviewed by an attorney proficient in contract law—before and during the hiring process. Well-crafted, legally vetted contracts protect both boards and CEOs from potential misunderstandings about the four basic components of employment—term of appointment, compensation (including salary and benefits), the evaluation process, and termination procedures—as well as any other terms that have been agreed on, such as specific duties, expense allowances, or working conditions. When feasible, boards and prospective CEOs should also have attorneys negotiate contracts— particularly first contracts—which can ease any reluctance either board members or CEOs may have about discussing terms more freely or in greater depth than would be possible in an interview. (For a comprehensive discussion of contracts, see Wallin, 2003.)

Perhaps more important than the responsibility of recruiting and hiring effective, peak-performing CEOs is that of supporting and retaining them. Foremost, boards need to create a supportive, enabling environment in which it is safe for the CEO to take risks and make tough and, sometimes, unpopular decisions (Boggs & Taylor, 2003, p. v). An employment contract that includes provisions for reviewing the CEO's performance annually (discussed in the next section) as well as the CEO's compensation, in light of new comparison data, is key to maintaining a supportive environment for the CEO. CEOs may need to convince a board of the importance of annual performance appraisal and an annual review of the employment contract.

EVALUATING CEOS

The CEO is the only college employee that the board should evaluate, and assessing the CEO's performance is one of the most important responsibilities of a community college board. Although a board has many opportunities to share evaluative comments informally during its regular interactions with the CEO, it is in everyone's best interests to schedule formal evaluations annually. The process and criteria for evaluations should be established by and mutually agreed on by both the board and the CEO at the outset of the CEO's tenure. CEOs need to know clearly what their boards expect from them. All too often, expectations are not made explicit, or individual board members may have different expectations for the CEO, which can create serious problems. Wise CEOs will draft goals and objectives and initiate discussion of them with the board. A goal-setting retreat can be an excellent vehicle for the board and the CEO to agree on expectations and directions for the college district.

CEOs are faced with conflicting demands, insufficient resources, hectic schedules, and long hours. In the evaluation process, CEOs should help boards understand that progress toward some college goals may take longer than expected when unforeseen challenges and other priorities emerge. Although maintaining a positive institutional climate is an important responsibility for a CEO, the board's evaluation of the CEO must be more than a reflection of the CEO's current popularity.

CEOs also may need to help their trustees understand that they alone are responsible for the annual evaluation of the CEO. Boards frequently receive requests from faculty and staff members to participate in the evaluation process, perhaps by submitting the results of anonymous employee evaluations. Boards may choose to accept and consider these materials and other input from the community or from others who interact with the CEO at the state or national levels, but the board should not delegate its important role in evaluating its CEO.

To assist the board in this annual evaluation, the CEO should prepare an end-of-year report that can serve as a self-evaluation. These reports document the activities and achievements of the CEO in maintaining positive community and college relationships, performing administrative duties, and providing educational leadership. A results section of the report should be devoted to the degree to which the goals set by the CEO and board have been accomplished.

The formal evaluation should result in a written performance record on which the board bases its annual review of the CEO's employment contract. A sample CEO evaluation policy and instrument are included in Appendixes A and B. Written evaluations should be sealed and placed in the CEO's personnel file for review only by regular members of the board or the CEO.

SELF-EVALUATION OF THE BOARD

Boards should evaluate their own performance periodically, and it is often up to the CEO to schedule this activity. The purposes of the board's self-evaluation are to clarify roles, enhance harmony and understanding among board members, and improve productivity of board meetings. The ultimate goal is to improve college operations and policies for the benefit of the community, the students, and the employees. It is often best to schedule the self-evaluation process at a special meeting or retreat. An outside facilitator might help keep the discussions productive. Board members should complete a short self-assessment beforehand to provide a basis for discussion. ACCT has a self-evaluation instrument item bank on its Web site under Center for Effective Governance. A sample self-assessment policy and form are included in Appendixes A and C.

ACTING AS BRIDGE AND BUFFER

Another important mission for boards is to act as both bridge and buffer between the college and the community (Nason, 1982, p. 35). As laypeople involved with the issues and concerns of the community, board members are in a position to communicate the community's educational needs to the college. According to Nason (1982, p. 36), trustees ought to be the antennae of the college. The board's voice can also be most persuasive in informing community members about the institution's programs and needs.

Colleges are seats of controversy (Nason, 1982, p. 37). Actions of students and faculty members frequently seem at odds with the expectations of at least part of the community. Yet academic freedom, freedom of thought and expression, and exploration are essential to the operation of an institution of higher learning. Board members can act as guardians to protect these freedoms and processes and explain why they are necessary. It is important for CEOs to remind trustees that institutional autonomy must be preserved. Board orientations should include information about the need to protect college culture, academic freedom, and the climate for learning and scholarship.

HEARING APPEALS

Boards are sometimes called on to hear complaints or appeals made by students, employees, community members, or disgruntled job applicants (Nason, 1989, p. 2). Some boards have policies that limit appeals to the board to alleged violations of college policy or law. Otherwise, they uphold administrative decisions that are made in accordance with law and their policies. An increasingly common practice is for boards to delegate hearings to an unbiased hearing officer who makes a report to the board. In the cases in which the board chooses to hear an appeal itself, the CEO should remind the board of its obligation to ensure that decisions are both just and legally defensible, with the board's basing its decision on the laws and policies that apply and the facts at hand. A complainant who is not satisfied with the board's or the administration's decision has the option of litigating through the courts or filing a complaint with a federal or state agency.

✳ Lessons Learned

MUTUAL TRUST AND RESPECT
Charlene Nunley
President, Montgomery College

Positive CEO–board relations are characterized by mutual trust and respect and function best in an environment of openness and honesty. CEOs must take the time to learn and understand trustees' interests and skills and give them the opportunity to apply them for the benefit of the college; trustees need to believe that they can make a real difference and that their efforts are valued. CEOs who regard board members as the wind beneath their wings rather than thorns in their sides are likely to foster more positive relationships with trustees.

The CEO and board should meet periodically in retreats or closed sessions to assess how their relationship stands. This assessment also should be a part of the board's annual performance review of the CEO.

PLANNING

CEOs must help boards recognize the complexity of the college and its operations, taking the long-range view, especially when the internal college community may be reluctant to do so. Boards should review the mission and vision statements of their colleges periodically. They and the CEO must ensure that the college community develops a useful master education plan that agrees with the college's mission and vision statements. The facility, staff, instruction, and student services plans must be integral parts of the master education plan for the college. CEOs can also involve trustees early in this process by engaging the board in discussion about the community's needs.

Boards have a special responsibility to future generations of students (Nason, 1982, p. 30). Whereas the internal college community is often focused on short-term problems, trustees and CEOs have an obligation to insist on long-term planning. Because colleges are human service institutions, they tend to focus on the problems of their people and can lose sight of facility needs. Here again, neither the board nor the CEO is responsible for drawing up long-range plans, but they must insist that the administration, faculty, and staff do so in terms that the board can approve. By devising a schedule for the development, periodic review, and approval of a long-range plan, the CEO can help the board meet this important responsibility. Long-range or strategic plans are defined as plans that embody the institution's key decisions about its mission, its agenda for the next 3 to 15 years to fulfill that mission, and its overall goals and objectives (Park, 1989, p. 4). Long-range plans should be designed to implement the college's shared vision statement.

RAISING FUNDS AND FRIENDS

Fundraising, long the purview of private colleges, has now become common in public colleges, and fundraising programs are growing in community colleges. In response to constraints on public funds, college boards and CEOs are making private fundraising a priority. Effective college development or advancement offices are staffed by professionals who are skilled in all aspects of fundraising, including capital campaigns and annual, deferred, and planned giving (Legon, 1989, p. 1). Although the advancement office usually coordinates public relations, government affairs, alumni affairs, and grant-writing activities, the CEO is often the public face of these efforts, and trustees need to show support for them because the internal college community may not easily recognize their comparative value to the institution. In private colleges, board members are expected to make substantial financial contributions and to solicit donations from others. In public colleges, a foundation board often serves this purpose.

Nonetheless, it is important for both governing board members and CEOs to support the private fundraising efforts of the college. They should contribute financially to the extent of their capacity: When the CEO and all board members contribute, they demonstrate the commitment necessary to persuade others to give. The board and the CEO must recognize their responsibility to see that the college's fundraising efforts are consistent with the mission and priorities of the institution (Legon, 1989, p. 3). Their attendance at fundraising events is important to demonstrate their support. Trustees should also be invited to attend occasional meetings of the college district foundation board to provide the link between the board that establishes the long-term goals and the one that raises funds and support. Involved and well-informed board members, willing to help the CEO by speaking to their colleagues and to groups about the college's goals, priorities, and accomplishments, provide a spirit and enthusiasm that lead to greater involvement in the college and support for its mission. CEOs can also ask trustees to put them in contact with influential community leaders and potential donors who may be persuaded to assist the college.

DEVELOPING PARTNERSHIPS

Many CEOs and trustees have found ways to stretch the resources of the college through partnerships with other agencies. Examples of partnerships include shared-use libraries, fitness centers, athletic playing fields, performing arts complexes, and special facilities created in partnership with business and industry. These partnerships also expand the influence of the college in the community and help promote economic development. Trustees often have the community and business connections to help the college make contacts necessary for developing these partnerships. CEOs can work with their trustees to help them identify the most important contacts. Trustees and CEOs must realize, however, that no single trustee, acting alone, has the authority to create a partnership.

✻ Lessons Learned

EDUCATION IMPROVES PERFORMANCE
Zelema Harris
President, Parkland College

Because I work with a supportive board that gives me candid assessments of my performance, I have been able to devote my energy to improving the performance of our institution and students, advocating for faculty and staff, and implementing policies affecting the future of the college. I doubt that my tenure and my performance at Parkland would have been long and successful if my time had been spent putting out fires and placating special interests.

One thing that I have found to be especially important in maintaining a positive and mutually beneficial relationship with my board is to spend time educating trustees about their roles and about critical issues affecting the college, which enables them to improve their performance. Furthermore, the more the board members engage in the college's planning and learn their roles, the better prepared they are to communicate with their constituents and support the president.

Some CEOs speak of being lonely at the top; fortunately I have not found this to be the case with my board. Parkland's trustees have expended their time and their energy to build a substantive relationship with me. It is not a prescribed relationship that is based on a formula or on management techniques but a human one based on mutual respect and caring. This relationship doesn't require us to compromise our values or beliefs. We have simply taken the time to get to know one another as people, and that has made all the difference.

ADVOCACY

In the competition for limited funds, CEOs and trustees should be spokespersons and advocates for their institutions. Some of the most important advocacy must be directed toward policymakers at the local, state, and federal levels. CEOs who brief their trustees regularly on legislative issues are a step ahead when a concerted effort is called for. In addition, CEOs would be wise to tap the political expertise on their boards. Boards and CEOs also need to be vigilant in monitoring the efforts of special interest groups that propose legislation that could hurt the college or its students.

Legislative advocacy does not begin when there is a need to lobby for or against a bill. Instead, it is necessary to develop a relationship with legislators and their staffs over time. CEOs should work with their boards to develop a legislative and communications advocacy plan so that all parties know their responsibilities and where to get needed information. Board members who are either publicly elected or politically appointed have an advantage in gaining access to legislators. It is also important for legislators to see the CEO and the board members as leaders who can sway public opinion. That means the CEO and board members must be visible in the community, and they must support community activities and attend community events. Writing opinion pieces for the editorial pages of local newspapers or participating in radio or television interviews on public policy issues is another way that CEOs and trustees can become influential advocates. CEOs can provide essential assistance to trustees who take up the challenge to write an article or an opinion editorial or to participate in a radio or television interview.

Although CEOs should never financially support candidates for their own board of trustees, they and their board members can contribute personally to the campaigns of candidates for other public offices. They may donate to candidates from any political party and provide them with information to help them build their campaign platforms on education issues. CEOs can also act to moderate candidate debates or forums. This kind of support and visibility often makes a difference in gaining access to busy legislators after the election. CEOs, however, should be cautious about publicly endorsing one political candidate over others, especially if the office is one that will influence the distribution of resources to the college or the appointment of college trustees.

Legislators and their staff members should be invited to the campuses to learn about the college, its programs, and its needs. They can be given a short campus tour and an opportunity to visit with students and faculty members. CEOs should make sure that legislators and their staff see the areas of campus that need improvement. Including trustees in these tours is an important way for them to be involved in advocacy and know the needs of their campuses.

In some instances, it will be necessary to mobilize the college community and college supporters to advocate for needed legislation. Trustees, foundation board members, and college advisory committee members can be very helpful by sending advocacy letters on their business letterhead. The CEO can improve the response rate of these college supporters by enclosing a sample letter and talking points with the request for assistance.

CEOs must take the lead both in communicating frequently with legislators at the local, state, and federal levels and in keeping the board members aware of important legislative issues. CEOs should also encourage trustees to build on their political connections as appointed or elected officials to advocate with state and federal policymakers. Communications with legislators should appeal to any interests these policymakers might have that are related to the college mission. When writing letters to legislators, CEOs should ensure that all board members receive copies. When legislators help, they should receive thank-you notes from the CEO, and trustees should be informed about the legislative assistance.

Chapter 4
Appointments and Elections

SEEKING CANDIDATES

When boards are appointed, the appointing agency may consult with the CEO or with current board members to seek suggestions for potential candidates. Because the CEO is employed by the board, it is probably not wise to lobby publicly for the appointment of one of its members. However, the CEO can suggest strong candidates and encourage the interest of leading citizens who are likely to make good board members. In any case, the CEO must become familiar with the appointing process and help others understand it.

As with other teams, the effectiveness of a board is enhanced when the backgrounds and interests of its members reflect diversity. It is also desirable for governing boards to be balanced by gender and to reflect the ethnic makeup of the community. Historically, college boards have been male-dominated and mostly White (Nason, 1982, pp. 56–57). Female and minority trustees bring important perspectives, styles, approaches, and sensitivities to the table (Ingram, 1988, p. 8).

Qualified candidates who would add depth and balance to the board should be exposed to the college and its programs. Affiliation with the college through service on an advisory committee or on a foundation board provides excellent experience for a potential member of the college's board of trustees. CEOs may want to encourage promising trustee candidates to serve on an affiliated committee or to help with fundraising.

ENDORSING CANDIDATES

In the case of an elected board, a CEO must never nominate, endorse, support, or donate campaign funds to one of the candidates. The CEO can encourage good candidates to consider board service at some point; however, the CEO needs to avoid the appearance of encouraging candidates to run against incumbent trustees and should not campaign publicly against a trustee or a candidate. The CEO can conduct an orientation session for the candidates, answer their questions, and supply information to them so long as all candidates are given equal opportunity. Forums for candidates are best organized by the board and held without the direct involvement of the CEO, although it is probably a good idea for the CEO to attend.

✳ Lessons Learned

SIX PRACTICAL TIPS FOR CEOS
Wayne Newton
Former Board Chair, Kirkwood Community College

- Don't take any job that doesn't feel good. CEO–board relations are like marriages. Your spouse will not change because you think you can make a difference.
- Introduce your board to the students early on, especially the new trustees. They need to be in touch with the community college mission.
- Showcase the faculty in positive ways. All too often, trustees see staff only through the eyes of the CEO or in the context of collective bargaining.
- Let the board see you double check the dinner ticket when you take them out to dinner. Don't make an issue of it, but they will appreciate your bean-counting skills.
- Insist that boards evaluate you and themselves. This is a forced conversation that can only strengthen the relationship.
- Be totally open to trustees. They can handle problems and perhaps even provide solutions. No surprises.

ORIENTING CANDIDATES

The best time to start orienting trustees is when they become candidates for the board. Candidates who are informed about the philosophy and organization of the district and the responsibilities and time commitment of trusteeship will have a better idea of what they may be getting into and will be able to run more informed campaigns. ACCT provides a checklist of information and activities on its Web site under the Center for Effective Governance. Activities may include the following:

- Inviting candidates to the college or district office for a presentation by the administration about the mission of the college district, long-term goals, and educational and support programs.
- Inviting candidates to attend board meetings to observe the proceedings and meet current members.
- Distributing sample board agendas and other written materials about trusteeship.

Orientation activities should show candidates that the district takes governing board membership seriously and that board members are expected to become contributing members of the college community as well as represent their constituencies. Care should be taken, however, not to patronize candidates. In some cases, they may be very knowledgeable about both the college and trusteeship.

STUDENT TRUSTEES

Some states have passed laws specifying that a student be a member of the college's board of trustees. Nason (1982, p. 59) has criticized the concept, because student trustees serve too briefly to master all they need to know and may not be on the board long enough to realize the consequences of their involvement. However, because many legislators have put students on boards in the belief that that this will ensure that students' viewpoints are considered when the board deliberates, CEOs would be well advised to meet with student trustees regularly and provide opportunities for orientation and development.

Student trustees are usually elected by the students at large and are obliged to represent students' perspectives to the board and to report and perhaps explain the board's actions to the student government. Student trustees usually do not have the same rights and responsibilities as publicly elected or politically appointed board members. Sometimes they are given an advisory vote, but they usually cannot make or second motions, and, in some states, they may not be allowed to participate in closed or executive sessions. Nonetheless, the wise CEO will treat the student trustee relationship with respect and work to help the student develop competencies as a trustee. The CEO's office, rather than the student affairs office, should be the point of contact for student trustees, just as it is for the other trustees. CEOs can refer to *Effective Student Trustees* (Kachiroubas, 2004) for information that they can provide to help their student trustees.

Chapter 5
Orientation and Development

SCOPE OF AUTHORITY AND RESPONSIBILITY

Boards need to be oriented and engaged in continuing education to help them meet their responsibilities in the manner in which they are legally empowered. CEOs need to ensure that their boards are prepared to exercise their authority appropriately in the course of their duties. Through its authority to set policies and attending to the long-range interests of the college, the board is in control of the systems that define the college and its character. Every orientation session should remind board members that they have no legal authority outside the meetings of the board. Comments by individual board members to the CEO, for example, should be taken as suggestions, whereas actions taken by the majority of the board in board meetings are directives for the CEO to implement. In talking with the press, an individual board member does not represent the board unless the majority of the board so directs in a board meeting. In some cases, the board chair has this authority as a matter of policy.

Trustees must pledge to devote sufficient time, thought, and study to their duties as board members so that they can render effective and creditable service. Specifically, this means preparing for board meetings (reading agenda materials, for example), attending them regularly, and asking questions. These responsibilities should be made clear to board candidates and newly elected board members.

Trustees and CEOs have the obligation to ensure the fiscal health of the college. Unfortunately, there are cases in which trustees and CEOs have yielded inappropriately to employee union demands or community pressure and increased the financial liability of the college irresponsibly. Whenever fiscal stability is jeopardized, the response must be some combination of increasing income and decreasing expenditures (Nason, 1982, p. 21). Unfortunately, laws in many states have greatly restricted the flexibility of local colleges in adjusting either expenditures or income. Authority to set tuition and property tax rates or to adjust the size of the contract faculty and staff differs by state. Nonetheless, local boards and their CEOs are held accountable for the proper fiscal management of the college.

Trustees and CEOs should also ensure that college funds are invested wisely. Unfortunately, some colleges and other public agencies have lost large percentages of their financial reserves or endowments because of risky investments. College funds must be protected, and investment strategies must be conservative.

Perhaps the most important nongoverning role for the board is ceremonial—representing the college at civic and charitable events and attending college functions such as commencements, program graduations, honors nights, and student performances. Faculty, staff, and students work hard to produce a play, prepare an art exhibit, or compete in an athletic event, and they deeply appreciate it when board members care enough to attend these events. Commencement ceremonies are especially important. CEOs need to provide dates of such events well in advance so that board members can fit them into their schedules.

A potential problem for a board member at these ceremonial events or college functions might occur when a student or member of the staff or community approaches the trustee to explain a problem or lobby for a special interest. On these occasions, the board member must understand that he or she has no legal authority as an individual trustee. The authority of the board is vested in the board as a whole and is exercised in the boardroom with other members of the board. An appropriate response in these circumstances is for the trustee to refer the individual to the college or district CEO, who can address the matter through appropriate channels. The CEO should remind board members never to try to solve an individual's problems with the college or commit to a position without hearing the recommendation of the CEO and staff in a board meeting.

CULTURE AND COMMITMENT

Although trustees may have backgrounds in business and industry, they must learn that colleges cannot be run like private business enterprises (Nason, 1982, p. 44). They should understand the authority they share with faculty and staff, the autonomy of the academic departments, the principle of academic freedom, the authority of accreditation commissions, the potential for intrusion on the part of state boards and legislatures, and limitations on the CEO's authority. State and federal laws restrict the freedom of judgment of both the CEO and the board. In addition, in most states, strict open-meeting laws govern the operations of the board. Actions that might be confidential in private business are open to public view in a tax-supported college. A wise CEO will be sensitive to the culture shock that awaits new trustees.

In issues of principle, it is important for the board and the CEO to convey clearly their commitment to particular philosophies. Student access to affordable and high-quality education is an almost universal value of the community college movement. However, access alone is not enough; the development of a culture that places learning at the heart of the institution must have the demonstrated support of the CEO and the trustees. Trustees and CEOs should also express their commitment to student equity efforts that measure and support the success of students regardless of their gender, race, ethnicity, and income. The CEO and board's strong support of the college's efforts to promote student access, success, diversity, and inclusion is essential if the college community is going to take its leaders seriously.

TRUSTEE ORIENTATION WORKSHOPS

When the composition of a board changes, even by one member, in many ways it is a new board. The CEO has an obligation to ensure that new members are oriented to their responsibilities, not only to enable the new member to become a productive and contributing trustee, but also to ensure the effectiveness of the CEO's leadership and the board's oversight. To prepare new board members to serve in this complex role, it is wise for the CEO to schedule at least one orientation workshop that includes all board members. An orientation workshop is also called for when a new CEO is appointed, to ensure that the CEO and the trustees have a common understanding of authority and responsibilities.

Sufficient time should be allotted in an orientation workshop to provide information about the college—its mission, vision, structure, and operations— and about trusteeship, ethics, and expectations for trustees. Continuing trustees can benefit from this refresher course and help answer questions for new trustees. Members of the CEO's executive leadership team can help by presenting information about how the major divisions of the college operate. The CEO should discuss the college's mission, vision for the future, long-range plans, and participatory committee system. If possible, the CEO should present an annual calendar of the board's scheduled actions and responsibilities so that new trustees will know what is expected at future meetings. The orientation should include a review of the board's function and how it is organized. If new board members are unfamiliar with campuses, walking tours should be scheduled and opportunities to talk with faculty, staff, and students provided.

Many experts suggest that an outside consultant or trustee from another institution, rather than the CEO, lead the orientation workshop discussion about trusteeship, ethics, and expectations. This has the advantage of allowing the CEO to be a participant instead of facilitator, and it spares him or her from having to lead the discussion on the relationship between the board and the CEO. A facilitator can use the college's code of ethics for trustees, which is now required for community colleges by most accreditation commissions (Boggs, 1993, p. 14; Smith, 2000, p. 217) as a basis for discussion. A sample ethics policy is included in Appendix F. Codes of ethics and written expectations for board members should be referred to frequently, not just at an orientation workshop. They should constantly guide the behavior of the board in its important work. Board ethics and codes of ethics are outlined thoroughly on ACCT's Web site.

Orienting a board to its responsibilities is not a short-term process. It takes time for a board member to understand the legal responsibilities of the position, the limitations imposed by open meetings laws, and the difference between policy setting and micromanagement. Understanding current issues facing the district, viewing those issues in a historical context, and making decisions with the long view in mind are even more complex. Advisory committees, organizational structures, collective bargaining, and accreditation may be unfamiliar issues to new trustees who do not have backgrounds in education.

PROFESSIONAL DEVELOPMENT

The education and development of trustees and CEOs should not stop after an initial orientation session. Conferences provide wonderful opportunities to learn from other CEOs, board members, and professional staff. Presentations reinforce effective CEO leadership and board governance and spark ideas to discuss with other board members. Another benefit of conference attendance is that it gives both CEOs and trustees the opportunity to understand that they are part of a larger community college movement that is meeting education and training needs in communities across the country. A more informed board is a better board.

An informal setting, such as a campus tour or a college event, can provide an excellent opportunity for a CEO to explain important issues and introduce a new board member to dedicated faculty and staff. One-on-one informal meetings or telephone conversations before board meetings enable new trustees to ask questions that may be difficult to raise in a more formal setting. One of the most important responsibilities of a CEO is to ensure that board members are informed by sending them information regularly, meeting with them individually, and calling them frequently. National and state trustee associations have as resources many periodicals and books about trusteeship, and CEOs should see that trustees have access to this literature. Ensuring that board members are educated about important issues facing the college not only elevates their role and expands their perspectives but also makes the CEO's job easier.

✳ Lessons Learned

TRUST-BUILDING STRATEGIES FOR CEOS
David Buettner
President, Fox Valley Technical College

The feedback I've received from the board members I have worked with over the years is all about trust. When I analyzed what I did to earn their trust, I came up with a set of strategies, which, although not intended to simply build trust, apparently did.

- Know each board member well. Understand their visions, values, and expectations. Private conversations, social interaction, and formal interactions, including regular retreats, all contribute to such understanding.
- Actively work toward supporting the board's agenda. When subtle facilitation fails to focus board members, advocate a point of view or idea to encourage them to speak up on their own.
- Use consensus-building skills to avoid any appearance of wounding individual board members as group decisions are made.
- Teach and facilitate good boardsmanship by being proactive in supporting board members' development. Case studies—fictional or drawn from the real-life experiences of other boards—are especially useful in retreat settings.
- Never put the board's trust in you at risk.
- Maintain your sense of direction even while respecting the direction that the board takes.
- Never let fear of failure, rejection, or upset of status quo prevent you from leading or suggesting direction or action.
- Be generous with recognition and stingy with blame.

RETREATS

It is often helpful to schedule occasional retreats or workshops away from the demands of a regular board meeting, where trustees and CEOs can plan, set goals, evaluate their progress, and assess the college's advancement toward realizing its vision for the future. As is the case with orientation workshops, an outside facilitator may make a retreat more productive. A side benefit of these more informal meetings is that they can engender a better understanding of roles and a better working relationship among members. Retreats can also be used to clarify CEOs' and trustees' expectations. Included in Appendix F is an update of an article on matching CEO and board expectations that is frequently used as a basis of discussion at retreats (Boggs, 1995a, pp. 8–14).

COOPERATION

CEOs should help trustees understand the importance of working with fellow board members and the CEO in a spirit of harmony and cooperation, despite differences of opinion that may arise during vigorous debates. Some boards and CEOs emphasize the importance of consensus or unanimous decisions. Divided votes of the board do not have to be a problem so long as a divided board does not emerge. Decisions must be based on all available facts about the issue at hand. Minority opinions should be respected, but the majority decision of the board must be supported. Board members should move on to the next issue without harboring hard feelings against other trustees. Abiding by these principles sets a positive example for the rest of the college to follow,

---

✳ Lessons Learned

RESPECT DIVERSE PERSPECTIVES
Pamela Transue
President, Tacoma Community College

Trust and respect form the keystone of positive relations between boards and CEOs. I value the diverse perspectives of board members offered within a climate of mutual respect. I do my best to keep the board fully informed of my activities, to tell them all the news, good and bad, and not surprise them. A clear understanding of the respective roles of board members and presidents is critical. Comprehensive orientation for new board members and an ongoing commitment to the board's development is essential. Beyond that, board members need to experience the life of the college through its activities, such as graduation ceremonies, to develop the passion for the mission that makes them effective advocates.

Chapter 6
Addressing Relationship Malfunctions

SPECIAL INTERESTS

Electing or appointing trustees with special interests to school and college boards is a recent and disturbing trend. Whereas all of us have special interests and religious or philosophical beliefs, trustees with special interests may have a specific agenda other than the best interests of the institution in mind. Board members who advocate religious beliefs or who bring nonrelated controversial issues to the table damage the very institution they are charged with protecting. Sometimes people run for boards for personal reasons or to start a political career. Some may seek to fire the CEO or desire to hold that position. Such trustees can be a challenge to a CEO. However, in many cases, a trustee who came to the position with a special interest can, over time, become an excellent and supportive member of the board.

Sometimes employee unions succeed in getting candidates elected or appointed to college governing boards. According to Ingram (1988, p. 9), all trustees have an obligation to remain independent of special interests or groups, and that includes employees. Trustees who feel an obligation to a particular internal group can hardly be unbiased in their decisions. In some cases, employees of one college are being elected to serve as trustees in another. Trustees sometimes have spouses or other relatives employed by the college they govern. Each of these situations presents opportunities for conflict of interest. The CEO and the other board members need to be aware of this potential and to advise particular board members of the appearance of such a conflict.

DISRUPTIVE BOARD MEMBERS

Sometimes the effectiveness of a board is limited because of a disruptive member. Examples range from a board member who does not prepare adequately for meetings, to one who always shows up late, to so-called rogue trustees who create significant problems for other board members and, more frequently, the CEO and college staff. Sometimes they are driven by special interests or their own agenda. Often, they distrust the CEO and college staff or other trustees. They do not respect the boundary between policy setting and administration, and they can cost the college unnecessary resources by demanding excessive information and placing other new requirements on employees.

A CEO will find a strong board chair to be most helpful when dealing with a problematic board member. A board chair or another influential board member can help by discussing concerns with the particular trustee in private. In many cases, CEOs will find that the most influential and helpful member of the board may not be the chair. There may be occasions in which the whole board may have to deal with a disruptive trustee or with one who is not living up to expectations or standards of ethics. Unfortunately, open-meeting laws in some states do not permit a board to address these issues in closed or executive sessions.

✳ Lessons Learned

DEEP-SIX YOUR EGO
E. Jan Kehoe
Superintendent-President, Long Beach Community College District

After 16 years as a CEO, I have come to believe that there is one thing that a CEO must do to establish and maintain good board relations and consequently open the way for a well-educated board: Deep-six your ego. By virtue of being selected as CEO, it is assumed that you are knowledgeable in your field. Boards are usually made up of members with different levels of understanding and knowledge of the community college, as well as a variety of motivations for being on the board.

I have served 27 board members. Each time a new member assumed office, the personality of the board changed. I have found that the best way to assimilate new members is to share knowledge, expertise, and expectations in a way that eliminates any elements of the CEO's ego, resulting in a board that not only supports the mission of the college but also the CEO. This advice may not always work, but with only one exception, I have always had supportive, knowledgeable board members.

ETHICS

Both the trustees and the CEO are public figures who must always be aware of ethical considerations involved in their actions and decisions—and not just those that take place in the boardroom, in the district office, or on campus. A trustee's or CEO's actions, even if they are unrelated to the college, will always be connected by the press and the public to the college. All too frequently, there are reports of CEOs or trustees who use their position and connections inappropriately to influence decisions that benefit family members or friends. Sometimes bids for college contracts are circumvented or employees are hired, reassigned, or even fired without going through established procedures. CEOs sometimes lose their jobs over mistakes that involve an insignificant amount of money or poor record keeping for financial reimbursements. Every decision that a CEO or board makes should be weighed against the college's code of ethics. Even the appearance of a conflict of interest or unethical behavior can create negative publicity and perhaps legal problems for the college as well as for the individual involved.

※ Lessons Learned

THE CEO MUST TAKE THE LEAD
Albert L. Lorenzo
President, Macomb Community College

Effective CEO–board relationships rest on a foundation of trust, candor, open communication, and mutual respect. When those elements are in place, the relationship can remain sound even when there are disagreements over how best to achieve institutional purposes. It is well understood that governing boards have the authority to establish college policy, but they also play a significant role in shaping organizational culture. For example, the values, attitudes, and beliefs evidenced by the board when making important decisions can easily become reflected in everyday institutional practices. Likewise, the highly visible relationship between the CEO and board can influence other critical relationships within the college. Simply put, the president cannot remain effective over time without a sound relationship with the board, and the president must take the lead in establishing and maintaining that relationship. The president must also be willing to admit that any sustained damage to the CEO–board relationship will ultimately cause damage to the institution itself.

SPLIT BOARDS

A split board is divided along philosophical or political lines resulting in consistent lack of unanimity in decision making and policy setting. In cases where a CEO has to work with a split board, it is important that the CEO not become politically aligned with one faction over the other. Political winds change, and a majority faction may find itself in the minority after the next election or appointment. These political shifts can trap a CEO. Drummond (2000, p. 2) cautioned CEOs against playing one trustee against another. Political turmoil among board members or between the CEO and board members weakens their ability to govern and is unhealthy for the college.

When a board is split over the service of the CEO, it is difficult for the CEO not to become aligned with the faction that supports him or her. However, even in this case, the CEO needs to support the work of the board as a whole. Sometimes it is possible to convert a nonsupporter. Drummond (2000, p. 1) has advised CEOs whose values may clash with some trustees to determine where there might be common ground and focus on those areas. If the split makes it impossible for the CEO to be effective, the best course of action might be to plan to step down and seek another position.

An experienced consultant or facilitator can sometimes help heal the hard feelings that often accompany a split board. An appeal must be made to the larger vision of doing what is right for the students and the college. Trustees do not have to be best friends to be effective, but all points of view should be respected.

OFFICES AND CAMPUS VISITS

The CEO's office should be the main point of contact between the board and the college. Having a separate board office on campus or hiring a separate staff for the board threatens the effectiveness of the CEO and invites the board to cross the line between governance and administration. Board members may choose to visit a campus occasionally to become better informed by talking with students and employees and sitting in on some classes and faculty and staff committee meetings. In these cases, the CEO can facilitate the visit and should always be informed before the visit. A trustee who does not inform the CEO about campus visits can, by this action, convey a lack of trust in the CEO. Meetings between a union and a board member during a collective bargaining impasse can damage the negotiations process. A board member who consistently attends internal college committee meetings runs the risk of inhibiting discussion and interfering with a process that is intended to bring informed recommendations to the board.

REJECTED RECOMMENDATIONS AND LACK OF UNANIMITY

Some CEOs view it as a personal defeat if the board does not support one of their recommendations. Surely, the board must seriously consider the CEO's recommendations; the CEO has studied the options and brings years of professional experience and personal knowledge of the college in making a recommendation. However, board members must make their decisions on the merits of the recommendation and not on who is making it. To do otherwise would indicate a weak board acting as nothing more than a rubber stamp for the CEO's wishes. Popcock (1989, p. 4) indicated that CEOs must supply solid recommendations, but they must accept the fact that boards will, on occasion, reject them. Consistent disregard of a CEO's recommendations signals that the board and CEO do not share common philosophies and both should be looking for a change.

EFFECTIVE ADMINISTRATION

Not all CEO–board problems are caused by difficult trustees. Sometimes the style or effectiveness of the CEO can be the root cause of issues that emerge with the board. Trustees expect a college to run smoothly and see too many college or employee problems as a red flag. An autocratic style may have

worked in the early days of community colleges, but it is unlikely to succeed in today's more collegial environment. The best CEOs are not threatened by employee involvement and facilitate the participation of people in making the decisions that will affect them. Faculty, staff members, students, and community members often serve on advisory community or college committees.
Because of the complexity of the organization, CEOs will have to delegate many decisions to others. Neither delegating nor letting others participate relieves the CEO and the board from the responsibility for administrating and governing the college district properly, however. The CEO and the board must retain the right to send a recommendation back to a committee or an administrator for further consideration or make a decision different from the one recommended.

Trustees often must make difficult and even unpopular decisions. They have a right to expect their CEOs to interpret their actions accurately and to support them to the public and to the college community. Of course, no CEO or trustee should ever be asked to support unethical or illegal actions. When confronted with a demand to act unethically or illegally, the CEO should ask the board to reconsider. If the board refuses to relent, the CEO should resign and seek another position.

VISIBILITY AND PRESTIGE

Many board members and CEOs enjoy the visibility and prestige that comes with college leadership. CEOs should always try not to overshadow their boards. A common mistake for CEOs is to pay too much attention to their own ego needs and not enough to the trustees who employ them. Trustees who view their CEO as arrogant or as a political threat will not be supportive.

CEOs must recognize that whatever benefits trustees receive are not nearly enough compensation for the hard work and long hours necessary to do a good job. Moreover, reelection or reappointment of trustees may depend on public recognition of the service provided. CEOs should take every opportunity to recognize the contributions of their board members and to acknowledge publicly their accomplishments and their leadership of local, state, and national organizations. CEOs need to give trustees the spotlight at appropriate times.

Of course, the most significant reward for CEOs and board members is the knowledge that they are contributing to the successful operation of a college and thereby improving both the community and the lives of students. CEOs should thank trustees regularly for their important civic contributions.

THE BOARD IS THE CEO'S HIGHEST PRIORITY
Pamila Fisher
Chancellor Emeritus, Yosemite Community College District

Developing and maintaining the best possible working relationships with the board of trustees must be the CEO's highest priority. This means that the CEO must respond promptly to calls, visits, inquiries, and requests. It also means providing frequent written updates on key issues and spending time with trustees individually or in small groups. I believe that it is also helpful to become well acquainted. The more a CEO knows about each trustee's goals, agendas, and even personal interests, and the more trustees know about the CEO's interests and goals, the easier it will be to work together. A smart CEO will encourage trustees to participate in state and national conferences and seminars and will always attend with them. This joint activity, probably more than any other one strategy, will not only increase the trustees' knowledge and perspectives, but also it will afford opportunity for informal contact between CEOs and boards, which helps build personal relationships.

Eventually a CEO may have to deal with one or more challenging, if not outright difficult, trustees. If this happens, it is helpful for the CEO to remember several things:

- Regardless of the trustee's behavior or differing opinions, he or she is still the CEO's "boss."
- Although it is very important for a CEO to address a trustee's inappropriate behavior, it is best to do it directly and privately.
- Only when a private conversation between the CEO and trustee does not work should the CEO involve the board chair or, if absolutely necessary, the entire board. Receiving negative feedback from one's peers can be threatening, and, even if other trustees support the CEO's viewpoint, any anger or hostility the trustee feels is likely to be directed at the CEO.
- If it becomes necessary to confront truly unethical or illegal behavior, CEOs would be wise to consider whether the issue in question is a matter of preference or principle before taking action, because the confrontation can do long-term damage to the relationship between the CEO and trustee.

I have worked with many excellent trustees in my career. When trustees with different agendas were elected to the board, it was exasperating for me when my efforts (e.g., keeping trustees informed, holding retreats, engaging consultants) did not work with some individuals. If positive strategies fail, a CEO must choose to find ways to work around or live with the situation. When that happens too often, or too many trustees are in disagreement, it is time for the CEO to look at alternatives. Not all situations are fixable, and a CEO's talents and energies just might be better used elsewhere.

Chapter 7
Communications

FREQUENCY OF MEETINGS

The frequency and length of board meetings varies by type of college and by state. Typically, community college boards meet once or twice a month for two to three hours. When meetings are more infrequent or shorter, it may indicate that a board is not meeting its responsibilities; trustees may be too disconnected from the college to govern it effectively. When meetings are more frequent or longer, that may indicate that a board is either unprepared for meetings or too involved in the administration of the college. In either case, these situations will present problems for the CEO unless they are corrected.

CONTACT WITH TRUSTEES

Some CEOs want all communications from board members to pass through them. The CEO can then contact appropriate staff members to gather information before answering a board member's questions. Other CEOs are comfortable with board members contacting other members of the executive leadership team directly, as long as the CEO knows about the contacts and their nature. If this is the case, it is important for members of the board and of the executive leadership team to keep the CEO in the information loop. Whatever the policy on trustee contact is, everyone should know it.

❋ Lessons Learned

COMMUNICATION IS KEY
Rufus Glasper
Chancellor, Maricopa County Community College District

Consistent and frequent communication is the key to effective CEO–board relations. Such relations are built on no surprises and the willingness to share information from multiple levels of the organization. As chancellor of a multicollege system, I cannot be aware of everything in as timely a manner as I would like; however, because the presidents and district public relations staff are encouraged and empowered to share information with the board, they assist me in minimizing or eliminating surprises for the board.

THE WEEKEND MEMO
J. William Wenrich
Chancellor Emeritus, Dallas County Community College District

The critical requirement of maintaining trust and respect between the board and the CEO depends heavily on adequate communication. All board members should be as informed as possible to achieve the goal of no surprises. One of the strategies I found most effective in my 28 years as a CEO was to send a weekend memo every Friday to all board members. In one to three pages, I devoted individual paragraphs to covering critical issues that had occurred that week, including achievements, failures, planning activities, or upcoming issues. This was an easy way to bring to the board's attention anything they needed to know before they heard it from someone else. The weekend memo also provided a record of my alerting the board to upcoming issues. My coverage was brief, but I always invited the board members to call me if they wanted more information. Sometimes writing weekend memos seemed a little tedious, but I believed it was important enough that I continued to write them until the week I retired.

CONTACT WITH NON-CEOS

CEOs cannot control contacts between board members and students, faculty, staff, and community members, but they can help inform board members about how they should deal with information relayed in these contacts. If a communication reveals a potential administrative problem, the board member should refer it to the CEO to address through appropriate administrative channels. If the person is trying to influence a board's decision on policy, the board member may choose to listen but should reserve judgment for the boardroom, where recommendations from faculty and staff committees and the CEO can be heard. Popcock (1988, p. 22) has cautioned board chairs to resist the temptation to respond to queries from faculty, students, administrators, and the news media until they are confident of the facts and have the CEO's agreement on the response. Board members should never commit to any course of action based on what they hear from people outside a board meeting.

GETTING TO KNOW TRUSTEES

Successful CEOs realize that it is important to get to know each trustee, what motivates the trustee to serve on the board, who the trustee knows in the community and at the college, and what interests the trustee has. Drummond (2000, p. 1) has advised CEOs to learn as much as possible about each board member. Visiting trustees at their places of employment is one way of showing an interest in them. Occasionally delivering board packets in person to a trustee's home or office provides another opportunity to interact with trustees.

Periodic lunch or breakfast meetings can also strengthen relationships while letting trustees know what issues are emerging at the college. CEOs, however, should respect open-meeting laws and not try to secure the board's consensus on issues outside a legal meeting of the board.

FRIENDSHIPS AMONG CEOS AND TRUSTEES

In the course of working together as a team, CEOs will, no doubt, develop friendships with board members. However, both CEOs and board members must make sure that friendship does not interfere with their professional responsibilities. Furthermore, CEOs and their staff members must never become involved in intimate relationships with members of their board. The CEOs who have allowed this to happen usually have paid for this mistake with damage to their careers or loss of their jobs.

WRITTEN REPORTS

CEOs often find it useful to prepare a regular, perhaps weekly, written report to the board to keep them informed about significant college-related issues and those that might be emerging. An important responsibility of the CEO is to protect the board against surprises and to ensure they are not the last to know about a college issue. Not many circumstances can be as embarrassing for a CEO as when a trustee hears about a problem from a reporter calling for comment. CEOs can keep the board informed via telephone as issues emerge, but sending a routine memorandum to the board—by mail, e-mail, or fax—forces the CEO to think about issues that the board needs to hear about. It is wise for CEOs to remember that, in most states, written materials provided to all board members are considered public records.

COMMUNICATIONS IN ADVANCE OF MEETINGS

Although board members decide what types of items to include on the agenda, they expect their CEOs to prepare materials for board meetings and provide a complete set of backup information. The CEO should ensure that the agenda materials arrive in time for board members to be able to study them. Board members should feel free to call the CEO should they have questions about agenda items. Alternatively, the CEO can call each board member routinely before meetings to find out if they have questions. This call gives the CEO the opportunity to answer quick questions and prepare the staff to answer more involved questions at the meeting. Without advance notice, staff members may be caught unaware and unable to respond appropriately at the board meeting. The CEO's call also provides an incentive to trustees to read the board meeting packets before the meeting. The CEO should not use a telephone call to advocate for a particular position. Arguments about the issues should be reserved for the boardroom.

NO SURPRISES IS A GOLDEN RULE
Robert G. Templin
President, Northern Virginia Community College

The most important lesson I have learned about maintaining positive CEO–board relations is that communication with the board has to be carefully thought through as a strategic effort rather than as a routine activity. Because most board members are not in day-to-day contact with the CEO's office, it is natural that communicating with the board tends to revolve around preparing for and following up board meetings. A conscious and consistent effort must be taken to think about the "white space" between board meetings when what is not communicated can become more important than what is, especially when an issue breaks into the news without warning. "No surprises" is a golden rule that applies at all levels of governance.

CLOSED OR EXECUTIVE SESSIONS

CEOs should remind board members that deliberations and discussions of the board, staff, and legal counsel in closed or executive sessions are not to be released or discussed in public without approval of the board by majority vote. Trustees need to know that information leaks from closed sessions, whether accurate or not, can damage the position of the college in negotiations or create significant legal problems for the college, CEO, or trustees. Open-meeting laws in most states restrict closed-session topics to those such as personnel or disciplinary actions, pending litigation, employee salary and benefit negotiations, honorary degrees, and land acquisition.

WHAT BOARDS NEED TO KNOW

Board members set policy based on the information they receive in board agendas and meetings. Thus, they need information that is accurate and reliable. After they approve policies, they need to ensure that they are implemented as intended. The tool that board members have to accomplish these tasks is the ability to ask the right questions. A common folly, according to Carver, is for boards to want to "know everything that is going on" (1990, p. 119).

Carver suggested that board members receive only three types of information: decision information, monitoring information, and incidental information (1990, p. 118). Decision information is information a board receives to enable it to take appropriate action. This information is not judgmental but is prospective in that it looks to the future and can be used to evaluate some aspect of the future. Monitoring information is used to gauge whether previous directions of the board have been satisfied. This kind of information is judgmental in that it measures performance and is retrospective in that it looks to the past.

Good monitoring information allows for a systematic survey of performance against criteria.

Carver defined incidental information as any information that does not support future decision making or monitoring past directions. According to Carver, most of the information presented at board meetings is incidental, and he warned that it often masquerades as monitoring information and implied that it is less valuable. Incidental information does, however, serve to educate boards about the college and its programs, connecting them to the mission of the institution.

Because trustees are proud of their colleges and the people who are part of the college community, it is important for the CEO to provide board members with information about the successes and achievements of the district, colleges, students, and employees. This practice makes it possible for the board to recognize employees and students appropriately. CEOs must be sure to share credit with others for district accomplishments.

Chapter 8

Termination of a CEO's Employment

T he most common reasons why a CEO leaves his or her position are career advancement, retirement, disability, or death. Termination can also occur because either the board or the CEO determines that a change of leadership is warranted. Whatever the reason for termination, both boards and CEOs have a responsibility—to each other as well as to the colleges and communities they serve—to ensure that the change in leadership takes place with minimal disagreement and disruption of college governance and community service.

The single most important thing that can be done to effect the smooth termination of a CEO's employment is to ensure that detailed policies and procedures have been established before hiring the CEO to guide the process and suggest ways in which to address potential problems. Specifically, these items should be in place:

- A signed CEO employment contract that includes a comprehensive termination clause that defines reasons for termination—for cause as well as without cause—and specifies what actions will be taken in either event. Such a clause will minimize debate about the board's and the CEO's rights and responsibilities at the time of termination (see Wallin, 2003, chap. 7).
- Formal evaluation tools that have been used regularly to set and monitor goals, objectives, and performance. Formal evaluations help ensure that written documents exist to support the board's assessment of the CEO's performance before termination, whether voluntary or for cause (see Wallin, 2003, chap. 4).
- A policy for giving notice of termination—either within the CEO employment contract or in a separate document. The policy should specify that the intention to terminate employment be communicated by either party at the earliest possible date and specify the amount of time each party expects to ensue between notification and termination, depending on the conditions of termination. If employment of a CEO is being terminated for cause, the board should communicate that decision to the CEO in a closed session. If a formal review process has been followed, notification of termination for reasons of performance should not take the CEO by surprise.

Even when seemingly clear policies and procedures regarding performance and termination have been established, misunderstandings can occur, and a CEO's termination can result in, at the least, negative publicity and, at the worst, litigation. When boards and CEOs find themselves involved in difficult or acrimonious circumstances, both parties should strive to air their grievances and negotiate a fair resolution before resorting to litigation. Litigation can harm everyone involved: Trustees at other colleges may be reluctant to hire a CEO who has taken legal action against a former employer; colleges with so-called troubled boards often have difficulty attracting qualified CEO candidates. And, most important, the confidence that a college or community has in the leadership of its board can be severely damaged or lost as a result of contentious CEO–board relationships, thus affecting the college's ability to raise funds, establish partnerships, and fulfill its mission.

When a CEO's termination does result in negative publicity, the CEO and board members should work together to draft a common statement to release to the press and the college community. As long as differences between the departing CEO and board exist, the media can be expected to exploit them to the detriment of the CEO, the board, and the college.

☼ Lessons Learned

LISTEN TO AND INFORM THE BOARD
Brice Harris
Chancellor, Los Rios Community College District

There is no substitute for open, honest, and frequent communication. I send my board members a weekly letter covering both good news and problematic issues. I talk to board members on the phone regularly and meet with them individually at least once each quarter. The board evaluates me in closed session twice informally and once formally each year.

My rule of thumb is to never surprise board members, and I never ask them to approve anything at the board table that I would not vote for myself. Yes, this approach is labor intensive, but with the exception of what goes on in our classrooms, there is nothing I do that is more important than keeping the board informed and listening to their advice and counsel. When I get tired of working with my board, it is time to get out of this job.

Chapter 9
Conclusion

The CEO is often in the best position to shape the effectiveness of the CEO–board team. CEOs can learn from the best practices of colleagues who are experienced and successful in the art and science of reporting to a board. In addition to the advice of 16 experienced and effective CEOs that appears in this book, Vaughn Sherman (1999, p. v), a founding member of the board of trustees at Edmunds Community College in Washington and past chair of the ACCT board, and Cindra Smith (2000, p. 72), director of education services at the Community College League of California, have both offered valuable advice that emphasizes the importance of ethics, open communication, evaluation, and development.

As the perspectives offered in this book show, to be successful, both CEOs and trustees must understand the role and function of a board, how they are structured, how policy differs from administration, how to organize and prepare for board meetings, why evaluation is essential, how orientation sessions and retreats can be used effectively, and how to work toward resolving problems.

Community colleges improve the lives of millions of people each year, but they are complex organizations, and, to be most successful, they require capable and stable leadership and governance. Ideally, the board of a community college district and its CEO should be viewed as a team that shares common philosophies and objectives. The effectiveness of one depends on the effectiveness of the other. Each has an important and complementary role to play, and they can be played more effectively if relationships are nurtured.

References

AACC Executive Search. (2006). *The risk you shouldn't take*. Available from www.aacc.nche.edu/executivesearch

Boggs, G. R. (1993). Making an ethical statement. *Trustee Quarterly*, 14–16.

Boggs, G. R. (1995a). Matching CEO and board expectations. *Trustee Quarterly*, 8–14.

Boggs, G. R. (1995b). The president and the board. In George A. Baker III (Ed.), *Team building for quality: Transitions in the American community college* (pp. 27–44). Washington, DC: American Association of Community Colleges.

Boggs, G., & Taylor, R. R. (2003). *The CEO contract: A guide for presidents and boards* [Foreword]. Washington, DC: Community College Press.

Carver, J. (1990). *Boards that make a difference*. San Francisco: Jossey Bass.

Drummond, M. (2000). Conflict or consensus? Seven steps to creating an effective board. In *Board focus* (pp. 1–2). Sacramento, CA: Community College League of California.

Ingram, R. T. (1988). Organizing the board. In R. T. Ingram & Associates (Ed.), *Making trusteeship work*. Washington, DC: Association of Governing Boards.

Kachiroubas, N. (2004). *Effective student trustees*. Washington, DC: Association of Community College Trustees.

Legon, R. D. (1989). *The fund raising role*. Washington, DC: Association of Governing Boards.

Nason, J. W. (1982). *The nature of trusteeship*. Washington DC: Association of Governing Boards.

Nason, J. W. (1989). *Trustee responsibilities*. Washington, DC: Association of Governing Boards.

Park, D. (1989). *The Board's role in planning*. Washington, DC: Association of Governing Boards.

Popcock, J. W. (1988). Maintaining effective chair-CEO relationships. In R. T. Ingram & Associates (Ed.), *Making trusteeship work*. Washington, DC: Association of Governing Boards.

Popcock, J. W. (1989). *The board chair-president relationship*. Washington, DC: Association of Governing Boards.

Sherman, V. A. (1999). *The essentials of board/CEO relations*. Washington, DC: Association of Community College Trustees.

Smith, C. J. (2000). *Trusteeship in community colleges: A guide to effective governance.* Washington, DC: Association of Community College Trustees.

Wallin, D. L. (2003). *The CEO contract: A guide for presidents and boards.* Washington, DC: Community College Press.

Appendix A
Sample Policy Statements
for the Evaluation of CEOs and Boards

EVALUATION OF CEOs

The evaluation of the CEO's performance shall be an ongoing and systematic process that culminates in an annual written review of the CEO by the board. The purpose of evaluation is to assess the CEO's performance based on the expectations stated in the CEO's job description as well as other goals and objectives developed annually between the CEO and board. Providing the CEO with a clear sense of direction, acknowledging good performance, and suggesting areas in which performance may be improved shall be the primary goals of evaluation; the ultimate goal is to ensure the efficient operation of the [college/system/district] for the benefit of students and employees.

Formal evaluation of the CEO shall occur annually and shall be the responsibility of the board. The process and criteria used shall be understood by and mutually acceptable to the board and the CEO, by means of a written assessment tool. The formal evaluation shall result in a written record of performance on which the board will base its annual review of the CEO's contract. Written evaluations should be sealed and placed in the CEO's personnel file for review only by board members or the CEO.

EVALUATION OF BOARD MEMBERS

Board members shall systematically monitor and self-evaluate their performance and submit an annual written self-evaluation to the board chair. The purpose of evaluation is to invite board members to self-assess performance in advancing organizational leadership, setting and monitoring policy, community relations, advocacy, CEO–board relations, and operational standards for the [college/system/district]; the ultimate goal is to ensure the efficient operation of the [college/system/district] for the benefit of students and employees.

Formal self-evaluation of the board shall occur annually and shall be the responsibility of the board. The process and criteria used shall be understood by and mutually acceptable to the board and the CEO, by means of a written assessment tool.

Individual self-evaluations shall be combined into an assessment document that shall be made available for discussion by the CEO and board members and shall be filed in the [college/system/district] office.

Appendix B

Sample CEO Evaluation Instrument

PROCEDURE

Evaluation of the CEO is to be based on performance of the duties outlined in the job description and on goals and objectives developed annually by the board and CEO. Instruments used in the evaluation will be reviewed periodically and may be revised by majority action of the board after discussion with the CEO. The board shall accept and consider relevant evaluation data submitted by internal and external constituencies.

- The CEO and the governing board shall mutually agree on the goals and objectives of the CEO annually. At the same time, the board shall review the responsibilities outlined in the job description of the CEO.

- The evaluation instrument is to be completed by each individual board member and submitted to the board President no later than the last regular board meeting in [month].

- The board President shall consolidate each board member's evaluation into one written report. The consolidated report shall be discussed and approved in closed session no later than the first regular board meeting in [month].

- The written report shall be delivered to the CEO at least one week prior to the last board meeting in [month]. At that meeting, the CEO shall meet in closed session with the board to discuss the evaluation.

- The evaluation report will be signed by all parties when final. A signed copy will be retained by the CEO, and a signed copy will be placed in the CEO's personnel file in a sealed envelope marked "To Be Opened Only by the Evaluee or a Voting Member of the Governing Board."

A. Relationship With the Governing Board

	Poor	Fair	Good	Very Good	Excellent
1. Keeps the board informed on issues, needs, and operations of the college [college/system/district].	❏	❏	❏	❏	❏
2. Offers professional advice to the board on items requiring board action, with appropriate recommendations based on study and analysis.	❏	❏	❏	❏	❏
3. Interprets and executes the intent of board policy.	❏	❏	❏	❏	❏
4. Supports board policy and actions to the public and staff.	❏	❏	❏	❏	❏
5. Maintains liaison between the board and college personnel to promote mutual understanding and respect.	❏	❏	❏	❏	❏
6. Provides the board with a written agenda and appropriate backup material in advance of each board meeting.	❏	❏	❏	❏	❏
7. Treats each member of the board in a professional manner.	❏	❏	❏	❏	❏
8. Responds quickly and effectively to questions from board members.	❏	❏	❏	❏	❏
9. Seeks and accepts constructive criticism of performance.	❏	❏	❏	❏	❏

Comments: _____

_____

_____

B. Community Relationships

	Poor	Fair	Good	Very Good	Excellent
1. Has gained the respect and support of the community as an educational leader.	❏	❏	❏	❏	❏
2. Has developed a friendly and cooperative relationship with the news media.	❏	❏	❏	❏	❏
3. Participates actively in community life and affairs.	❏	❏	❏	❏	❏
4. Works effectively with public and private agencies.	❏	❏	❏	❏	❏
5. Attends to the concerns and opinions of all groups and individuals.	❏	❏	❏	❏	❏

Comments: _____

_____

_____

C. STAFF AND PERSONNEL RELATIONSHIPS

	Poor	Fair	Good	Very Good	Excellent
1. Develops and executes sound personnel procedures and practices.	❏	❏	❏	❏	❏
2. Promotes positive staff morale and employee loyalty.	❏	❏	❏	❏	❏
3. Delegates authority to staff members appropriate to the position each holds.	❏	❏	❏	❏	❏
4. Recruits and assigns the best available personnel in terms of their competencies.	❏	❏	❏	❏	❏
5. Operates in a collegial mode; encourages participation of appropriate staff members and groups in planning, procedures, and policy interpretations.	❏	❏	❏	❏	❏
6. Evaluates performance of staff members, giving commendation for good work as well as constructive suggestions for improvement.	❏	❏	❏	❏	❏
7. Treats all personnel fairly, without favoritism or discrimination, while insisting on performance of duties.	❏	❏	❏	❏	❏
8. Takes an active role in the development of salary schedules and fringe benefits for all personnel and recommends to the board the levels that, within budgetary limitations, will best serve the interests of the [college/system/district].	❏	❏	❏	❏	❏
9. Meets periodically with employee and student groups to maintain open communication and to address concerns in a timely manner.	❏	❏	❏	❏	❏

Comments: _____

_____

_____

D. Administration

1. Organizes the staff so that decision making may take place at appropriate levels.   Poor ❏   Fair ❏   Good ❏   Very Good ❏   Excellent ❏

2. Periodically reviews and reorganizes staff duties and responsibilities to take full advantage of the staff's special competencies and interests.   ❏   ❏   ❏   ❏   ❏

3. Has developed a system that ensures that all significant activities or duties are performed regularly or administered promptly.   ❏   ❏   ❏   ❏   ❏

4. Encourages research and creativity among employees.   ❏   ❏   ❏   ❏   ❏

5. Periodically informs the board of the status of various programs of the [college/system/district].   ❏   ❏   ❏   ❏   ❏

Comments: _____

_____

_____

E. Educational Leadership

1. Implements the [college/system/district]'s philosophy of education.   Poor ❏   Fair ❏   Good ❏   Very Good ❏   Excellent ❏

2. Represents the [college/system/district] at state, local, and national meetings.   ❏   ❏   ❏   ❏   ❏

3. Speaks well in front of large and small groups, expressing ideas in a logical and forthright manner.   ❏   ❏   ❏   ❏   ❏

4. Writes clearly and concisely.   ❏   ❏   ❏   ❏   ❏

5. Encourages and inspires the college staff to continue to improve educational programs and services.   ❏   ❏   ❏   ❏

6. Fosters and supports excellence in educational programs and standards.   ❏   ❏   ❏   ❏   ❏

Comments: _____

_____

_____

F. BUSINESS AND FINANCE

	Poor	Fair	Good	Very Good	Excellent
1. Supervises operations, insisting on competent and efficient performance.	❑	❑	❑	❑	❑
2. Determines that funds are spent wisely and that adequate control and accounting are maintained.	❑	❑	❑	❑	❑
3. Evaluates the financial needs of the [college/system/district] and prepares an appropriate annual budget.	❑	❑	❑	❑	❑

Comments: _____

_____

_____

G. PERSONAL QUALITIES

	Poor	Fair	Good	Very Good	Excellent
1. Maintains high standards of ethics, honesty, and integrity in all personal and professional matters.	❑	❑	❑	❑	❑
2. Defends principle and conviction in the face of pressure and partisan influence.	❑	❑	❑	❑	❑
3. Earns respect among professional colleagues.	❑	❑	❑	❑	❑
4. Devotes sufficient time and energy to the job.	❑	❑	❑	❑	❑
5. Demonstrates the ability to work well with individuals and groups.	❑	❑	❑	❑	❑
6. Exercises good judgment and appropriate collegial processes in arriving at decisions.	❑	❑	❑	❑	❑
7. Maintains poise and emotional stability in the full range of professional activities.	❑	❑	❑	❑	❑
8. Is customarily suitably attired and well-groomed.	❑	❑	❑	❑	❑
9. Thinks well when faced with an unexpected or disturbing turn of events.	❑	❑	❑	❑	❑
10. Maintains professional development by reading, coursework, conference attendance, work on professional committees, visiting other [college/system/district]s, and meetings with other CEOs.	❑	❑	❑	❑	❑

Comments: _____

_____

_____

H. GOALS AND OBJECTIVES

	Poor	Fair	Good	Very Good	Excellent

Has worked to attain the goals and objectives that
were mutually set. ❏ ❏ ❏ ❏ ❏

Comments: _____

_____

_____

I. OVERALL RATING

Commendations: _____

_____

_____

Recommendations: _____

_____

_____

General Comments: _____

_____

_____

Signatures: _____

CEO: _____

Board Chair: _____

Board Vice Chair: _____

Board Secretary: _____

Board Member [include individual signature lines for each]:

_____

Date of Evaluation: _____

Appendix C

Sample Self-Evaluation Instrument for Boards

Instructions: Please complete the following evaluation instrument of the functioning of the board as a whole by marking the appropriate response.

A. BOARD ORGANIZATION/LEADERSHIP

A strong, effective board helps create a strong, effective institution by focusing on its own unique responsibilities.

	Strongly Agree	Agree	Neither Agree nor Disagree	Disagree	Strongly Disagree
1. In general, board meetings are conducted in an orderly, efficient manner that allows for sufficient discussion.	❏	❏	❏	❏	❏
2. The board operates as a unit.	❏	❏	❏	❏	❏
3. Board members uphold the final majority decision of the board.	❏	❏	❏	❏	❏
4. Meeting agenda items contain sufficient background information and recommendations for the board.	❏	❏	❏	❏	❏
5. The board understands its roles and responsibilities.	❏	❏	❏	❏	❏
6. The board adheres to its roles and responsibilities.	❏	❏	❏	❏	❏
7. The board maintains confidentiality of privileged information.	❏	❏	❏	❏	❏
8. The board operates ethically without conflict of interest.	❏	❏	❏	❏	❏
9. Board meetings allow appropriate input from staff, students, and community.	❏	❏	❏	❏	❏
10. The board works to achieve the [college/system/ district]'s goals and objectives.	❏	❏	❏	❏	❏
11. Board meetings comply with state laws.	❏	❏	❏	❏	❏

Comments: _____

_____

_____

B. POLICY

The most important board responsibility is to make good policy that provides guidance for [college/system/district] staff.

	Strongly Agree	Agree	Neither Agree nor Disagree	Disagree	Strongly Disagree
12. The board critically reviews its policies as they are developed.	❑	❑	❑	❑	❑
13. The board focuses on policy in its discussions.	❑	❑	❑	❑	❑
14. The board recognizes the difference between its policy role and the roles of the CEO and staff.	❑	❑	❑	❑	❑
15. The board, through the CEO, receives advice and recommendations from faculty, staff, and students in developing educational policy.	❑	❑	❑	❑	❑
16. The board is appropriately involved in defining the vision, mission, and goals.	❑	❑	❑	❑	❑
17. The board makes its decisions based on what is best for students and the community.	❑	❑	❑	❑	❑
18. The board recognizes and values staff and student diversity in policies and decisions.	❑	❑	❑	❑	❑
19. The board sets priorities in conjunction with the CEO	❑	❑	❑	❑	❑
20. The board is familiar with the general strategic and master plans of the institution.	❑	❑	❑	❑	❑

Comments: _____

_____

_____

C. COMMUNITY RELATIONS/ADVOCATING FOR THE [COLLEGE/SYSTEM/DISTRICT]

The board governs on behalf of the public and advocates on behalf of the college/system/district].

	Strongly Agree	Agree	Neither Agree nor Disagree	Disagree	Strongly Disagree
21. Board members act on behalf of the community.	❑	❑	❑	❑	❑
22. The board actively seeks to understand community and regional needs and expectations.	❑	❑	❑	❑	❑
23. Board members maintain effective relationships with community leaders.	❑	❑	❑	❑	❑
24. The board supports the development of educational partnerships with community agencies, businesses, and local government, where appropriate.	❑	❑	❑	❑	❑
25. The board recognizes and celebrates positive accomplishments of the [college/system/district].	❑	❑	❑	❑	❑

C. COMMUNITY RELATIONS/ADVOCATING FOR THE [COLLEGE/SYSTEM/DISTRICT] (CONT'D)

The board governs on behalf of the public and advocates on behalf of the college/system/district].

	Strongly Agree	Agree	Neither Agree nor Disagree	Disagree	Strongly Disagree
26. The board actively supports the mission and values of the [college/system/district].	❑	❑	❑	❑	❑
27. Board members support the [college/system/district] by attending various events.	❑	❑	❑	❑	❑
28. The board helps educate the local community about community college needs and causes.	❑	❑	❑	❑	❑
29. Board members actively seek to understand state and national educational policy issues.	❑	❑	❑	❑	❑
30. The board advocates [college/system/district] interests to regional, state, and national agencies and legislators.	❑	❑	❑	❑	❑
31. The board actively seeks political and civic support for the [college/system/district].	❑	❑	❑	❑	❑
32. The board works to build a positive image of the [college/system/district] in the community.	❑	❑	❑	❑	❑

Comments: _____

_____

_____

D. BOARD/CEO RELATIONS

The CEO is the primary agent of the board, carries out board policies, and provides educational leadership.

	Strongly Agree	Agree	Neither Agree nor Disagree	Disagree	Strongly Disagree
33. The board and the CEO have a positive, cooperative relationship.	❑	❑	❑	❑	❑
34. The board provides a high level of support to the CEO.	❑	❑	❑	❑	❑
35. The board maintains open communication with the CEO.	❑	❑	❑	❑	❑
36. The board annually develops goals and objectives that are used in the evaluation of the CEO.	❑	❑	❑	❑	❑
37. The board understands the role of the CEO as the link between the board and staff.	❑	❑	❑	❑	❑

Comments: _____

_____

_____

E. STANDARDS FOR [COLLEGE/SYSTEM/DISTRICT] AND COLLEGE OPERATIONS AND PERFORMANCE

The board holds the [college/system/district] accountable and establishes a climate in which learning is valued.

	Strongly Agree	Agree	Neither Agree nor Disagree	Disagree	Strongly Disagree
38. The board is knowledgeable about the educational programs and services of the [college/system/district].	❑	❑	❑	❑	❑
39. The board understands the fiscal condition of the [college/system/district].	❑	❑	❑	❑	❑
40. The board understands the budget document.	❑	❑	❑	❑	❑
41. The board establishes clear parameters for negotiating, meeting, and conferring with employee groups.	❑	❑	❑	❑	❑
42. The board demonstrates a concern for the success of all students.	❑	❑	❑	❑	❑
43. The board is involved in the accreditation process.	❑	❑	❑	❑	❑
44. The board monitors performance related to its policies for facilities development, maintenance, and appearance.	❑	❑	❑	❑	❑
45. The board monitors performance related to its policies on fiscal management.	❑	❑	❑	❑	❑
46. The board understands the financial audit and its recommendations.	❑	❑	❑	❑	❑
47. The board ensures that a collegial governance structure is used to provide access to and input from all constituencies so that decisions may be made in a timely manner.	❑	❑	❑	❑	❑

Comments: _____

_____

_____

Overall Comments: _____

_____

_____

Please provide any narrative feedback you would like included as part of this self-assessment.

_____

_____

Board Member Name _____

Appendix D
Sample Code of Ethics for CEOs and Boards

As a member of the governing board of [name of college/system/district], I will perform my duties in accordance with my oath of office. I am committed to serving the educational needs of the citizens of the [college/system/district]. My primary responsibility is to provide learning opportunities to all students regardless of their race, sex, color, age, religion, ancestry, creed, national origin, political beliefs, marital status, sexual orientation, medical condition, physical disability, or Vietnam-era veteran status.

It is my further responsibility to

- Devote time, thought, and study to my duties as a community college board member so that I may render effective and creditable service.

- Work with my fellow board members in a spirit of harmony and cooperation in spite of differences of opinion that may arise during vigorous debates of points at issue.

- Base my personal decisions on all available facts in each situation, vote my honest conviction in every case unswayed by partisan bias, and abide by and uphold the final majority decision of the board.

- Remember at all times that as an individual I have no legal authority outside the meetings of the board and conduct my relationships with college staff, students, the local citizenry, and the media on that basis.

- Be aware that I am responsible to all residents in the [college/system/district] and not solely to those who [elected/appointed] me. The authority delegated to me by the voters must be exercised with as much care and concern for the least influential as for the most influential member of the community.

- Resist every temptation and outside pressure to use my position as a community college board member to benefit either myself or any other individual or agency apart from the total welfare of the [college/system/district].

- Recognize that it is as important for the board to understand and evaluate the educational program of the college as it is to plan for the business of college's operation.

- Bear in mind under all circumstances that the board is legally responsible for the effective operation of the [college/system/district]. Its primary function is to establish the policies by which the [college/system/district] is to be administered. The board shall hold the CEO and his or her staff responsible for the administration of the educational program and the conduct of college business.

- Welcome and encourage the active involvement of students, employees, and residents in the [college/system/district] with respect to establishing policy on current college operations and proposed future developments and consider their views in my deliberations and decisions as a board member.

- Recognize that deliberations of the board in closed session are not mine to release or discuss in public without the approval of the board by majority vote.

- Avail myself of opportunities to enhance my potential as a board member through participation in educational conferences, workshops, and training sessions offered by local, state, and national organizations.

- Be informed about the actions and positions of state and national community college trustees' associations.

- Strive to provide the most effective community college board service of which I am capable, in a spirit of teamwork and devotion to public education as the greatest instrument for the preservation and perpetuation of our representative democracy.

Appendix E
Matching CEO and Board Expectations

WHAT BOARD MEMBERS EXPECT OF CEOS

- Be honest in dealings with board members.
- Keep all board members informed of issues, needs, and operations of the [college/system/district].
- Schedule orientation retreats for the board shortly after new members are seated.
- Be available to answer questions from board members.
- Do not consistently side with one particular board member or with any faction of the board.
- Accept that a consensus of the board may not always be possible.
- Make recommendations on all issues that require action by the board.
- Provide guidance to the board in the development of goals.
- Provide adequate and timely information for board meeting agenda.
- Be committed to the effective operation of the [college/system/district].
- Find ways to make things happen (ethically).
- Involve board members and constituents appropriately in decision making.
- Be visible on campus, in the community, and in statewide and national forums.
- Help board members develop parameters for collective bargaining with employees.
- Inform the board about the accomplishments of students, employees, and the [college/system/district].
- Inform the board about important legislative issues at the local, state, and federal levels.
- Provide visible public support for board members.
- Support the board's policies and actions to staff and the public.

WHAT CEOS EXPECT OF BOARD MEMBERS

- Provide the CEO with a clear understanding of the board's expectations.
- Regularly evaluate the CEO.
- Recognize the distinction between policy setting and operations.
- Work with fellow board members and the CEO in a spirit of harmony and cooperation.

- Provide visible public support for the CEO.
- Base decisions on what is best for the [college/system/district] not on special interests.
- Refer complaints and suggestions to the CEO.
- Ensure that the CEO is the primary contact with the [college/system/district].
- Protect the mission of student learning.
- Protect the long-term interests of the [college/system/district].
- Prepare adequately for board meetings.
- Maintain appropriate confidentiality.
- Avoid public criticism of the CEO.
- Address inappropriate behavior of fellow board members.
- Recognize the CEO and other college staff for local, statewide, and national leadership roles and achievements.
- Support the professional involvement and development of the CEO.
- Review the CEO's employment contract annually to ensure that provisions are fair and competitive.
- Act responsibly in terminating a CEO's employment.

Note. Adapted from "Matching CEO and Board Expectations," by G. R. Boggs, 1995, Trustee Quarterly, Issue 4, *pp. 8–14.*

About the Author

George R. Boggs is president and chief executive officer of the American Association of Community Colleges (AACC), based in Washington, DC. AACC represents more than 1,100 associate degree–granting institutions and more than 11 million students. Boggs previously served as faculty member, division chair, and associate dean of instruction at Butte College in California, and for 15 years he served as the superintendent/president of Palomar College in California. He served as a member of the Committee on Undergraduate Science Education of the National Research Council and has served on several National Science Foundation panels and committees. He holds a bachelor's degree in chemistry from The Ohio State University, a master's degree in chemistry from the University of California at Santa Barbara, and a PhD in educational administration from The University of Texas at Austin.

Index